The Cheyenne

Hunter-Gatherers of the Northern Plains

by Mary Englar

Consultant:
Rick Juliani, M.A.
Educator and Curriculum Coordinator
Hopi Day School
Kykotsmovi, Arizona

Capstone
press
Mankato, Minnesota

Capstone Press,
151 Good Counsel Drive, P.O. Box 669, Mankato, Minnesota 56002.
www.capstonepress.com

Library of Congress Cataloging-in-Publication Data
Englar, Mary.
    The Cheyenne: Hunter-gatherers of the northern plains/by Mary
Englar.
        v. cm.—(American Indian nations)
    Includes bibliographical references and index.
    Contents: Who are the Cheyenne?—Traditional life—Change comes to
the Cheyenne—The Cheyenne today—Sharing the traditions—Map: The
Cheyenne past and present—Recipe: Cheyenne batter bread—Cheyenne
timeline
    ISBN 0-7368-2178-3 (hardcover)
    ISBN 0-7368-4813-4 (paperback)
    1. Cheyenne Indians—Juvenile literature. [1. Cheyenne Indians.
2.Indians of North America—Great Plains.] I. Title. II. Series.
E99.C53E64 2004
978.004'973—dc21   2002156006

Editorial Credits

Blake A. Hoena and Charles Pederson, editors; Kia Adams, series designer;
Molly Nei, book designer and illustrator; Kelly Garvin, photo researcher;
Karen Risch, product planning editor

Cover Photos

Cheyenne Indian standing next to tepee, Denver Public Library; bow and
arrow (inset), Colorado Historical Society

Photo Credits

Kit Breen, 4, 40; The Denver Public Library, 8, 18; Marilyn "Angel" Wynn,
11, 29, 36, 44, 45; Library of Congress, 13, 22; Smithsonian Institution,
National Anthropological Archives, 14; Photo Disc
Inc., 16–17; Capstone Press/ Gary Sundermeyer, 17; Colorado Historical
Society, 19; Photo Network/ Margo Taussig Pinkerton, 21; Stock Montage
Inc./Newberry Library, 24; Stock Montage Inc., 26; Archives and
Manuscripts Division of the Oklahoma Historical Society, 30; Corbis, 33, 35;
Raymond Bial, 39; photo courtesy of Suzan Shown Harjo, 43

2 3 4 5 6 08 07 06 05

Table of Contents

Features

Modern Cheyenne are descendants of a powerful American Indian nation.

Chapter One

Who Are the Cheyenne?

The Cheyenne (shye-EN) were once a powerful American Indian nation. They fought other Indians as well as American settlers and were respected for their battle skills. The Cheyenne also were known for their horsemanship and beautiful arts.

European explorers learned about the Cheyenne from the Lakota Sioux (SOO). The Lakota called the neighboring Cheyenne "Shahiyena." In the Lakota language, this word means "people who speak a different language." In English, the name became Cheyenne. The Cheyenne call themselves Tsistsistas, which means "the people."

Beginning in the late 1600s, the Cheyenne way of life changed. The Cheyenne originally farmed and hunted in the woods near the western Great Lakes. They left the area for present-day North Dakota and South Dakota. They were interested in obtaining horses to use for hunting and for defending themselves from their enemies.

By about 1800, the Cheyenne had stopped farming. They traveled the Great Plains in search of buffalo for food. The Cheyenne followed the buffalo from Montana in the north to Texas in the south. The Cheyenne lived mainly in present-day eastern Colorado and western Kansas.

Today, the Cheyenne are split into two groups. The Northern Cheyenne live on a reservation near Lame Deer in southern Montana. The Southern Cheyenne share tribal land with the Southern Arapaho near Concho, Oklahoma. Both Northern and Southern Cheyenne share language, religion, and customs. They consider themselves one people.

The 2000 U.S. Census counted 11,191 people as Cheyenne. About half of them live on or near Indian lands in Montana and Oklahoma. Others have moved to large cities to continue their education and to find work.

The Cheyenne live much like other Americans. They are ranchers, farmers, teachers, and politicians. They also work to protect their land and keep their traditions alive.

The Cheyenne Past and Present

MONTANA
NORTH DAKOTA
SOUTH DAKOTA
MINNESOTA
N
W
E
S
OKLAHOMA
Legend
Cheyenne Lands before 1800
Modern Cheyenne Lands
Modern United States
Modern Mexico
Scale
Miles
0 25 50 75 100
0 25 50 75 100
Kilometers
MEXICO
Gulf of Mexico

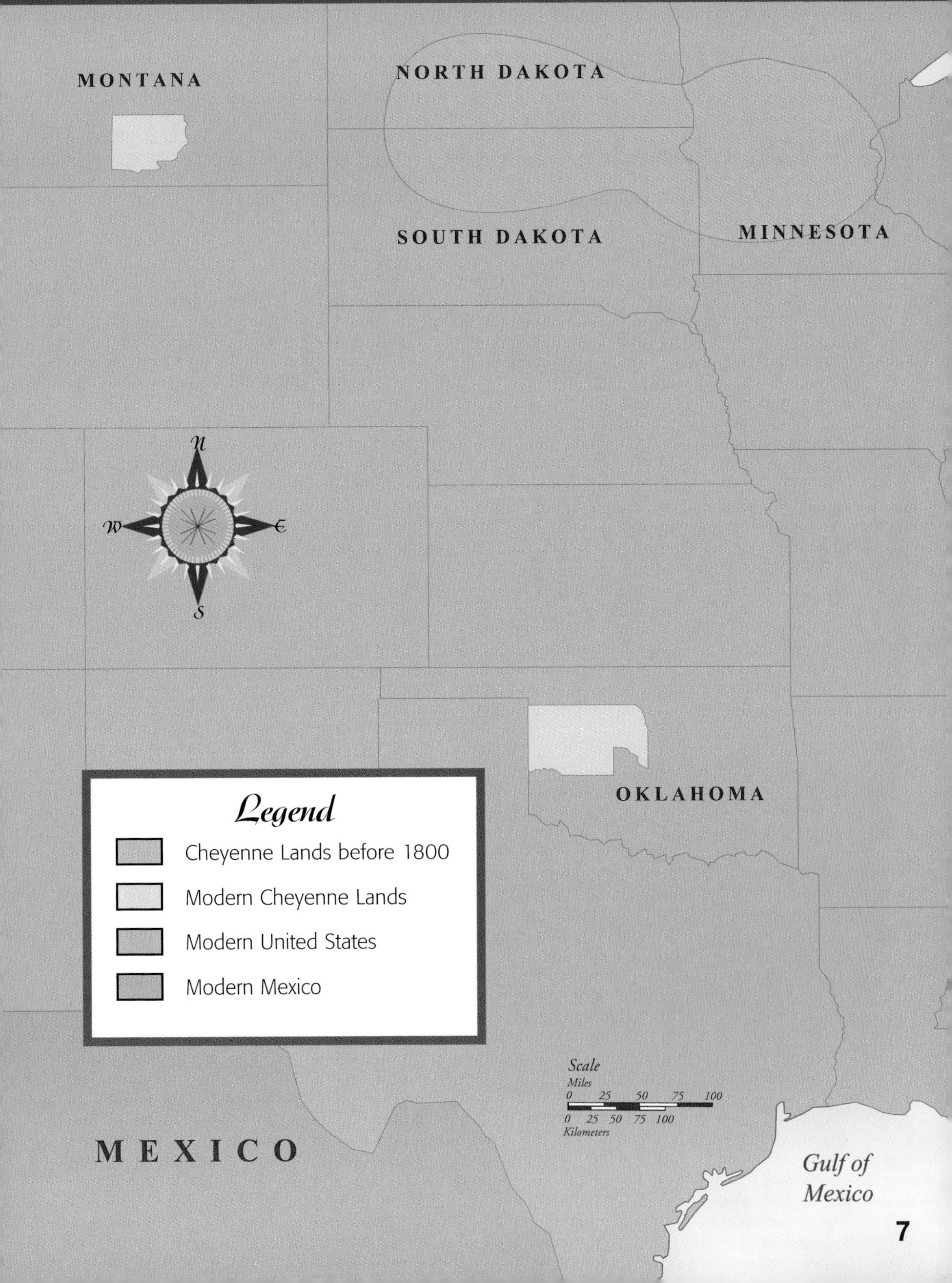

The Cheyenne lived in tepees after moving to the
Great Plains.

Chapter Two

Traditional Life

Before the Cheyenne moved to the Great
Plains, they lived in villages along the
rivers and lakes of Minnesota. They lived
in round houses covered with tree bark.

The Cheyenne had many sources of
food. They grew corn and other vegetables.
They gathered wild rice in swampy areas.
The Cheyenne hunted deer, bear, elk, and
turkeys. They also traveled to the Great
Plains each year to hunt buffalo.

By about 1800, the Cheyenne had
quit farming and left their permanent
villages. They became nomadic hunters
who followed buffalo herds from place to

place. They also traveled south to trade for horses and other goods from Indians and other people in the southwest.

Cheyenne travels changed with the seasons. During winter, they traveled in small family groups of 20 to 50 people. In spring, the Cheyenne gathered in large groups for ceremonies and the first buffalo hunt of the year. After the summer hunts, bands of 300 to 350 people moved to river valleys to find clean water and grass for their horses. In early winter, the bands then split again into family groups.

At one time, 10 bands of Cheyenne lived in different areas of the plains. Each band was made up of several large, extended families. An extended family included aunts, uncles, grandparents, and cousins, as well as brothers, sisters, and parents. Each band lived, worked, and hunted as a group.

Tepees

On the Great Plains, the Cheyenne lived in tentlike shelters called tepees. They learned to make tepees from other plains Indians. Tepees were practical because they were easy to put up and take down. A tepee was made of a frame of long, straight tree trunks. Buffalo skins covered the frame.

Cheyenne tepees were different from other plains Indians' tepees. Cheyenne women rubbed the buffalo hides with white clay or a mineral called gypsum. These materials made the tepees bright white. Travelers could tell from a distance that they were seeing a Cheyenne village.

In each village, a few tepees had brightly painted designs or pictures. Painted tepees usually held religious items.

Horses

Horses changed the Cheyenne way of life. Traditionally, the Cheyenne traveled on foot. By about 1800, they had traded for

In this photo, a Cheyenne girl sits near the tepees of her village.

horses from other plains Indians. Hunters could travel farther on horseback than they could on foot. Horses could keep up better with running buffalo. The Cheyenne could kill many more buffalo on horseback than on foot. Horses allowed the Cheyenne to follow buffalo herds around the Great Plains.

The Cheyenne moved camp as often as every five days from spring until winter. Horses could carry large loads when the Cheyenne moved. The horses carried tepees, household goods, and people. With horses, the Cheyenne could move as far as 20 miles (32 kilometers) a day. On foot, they could move only a few miles or kilometers.

The Cheyenne wanted as many horses as possible. The number of horses a man owned showed his importance. The Cheyenne stole horses, traded for them, or won them in battle. Most bands had at least one horse for every person. Chiefs and warriors sometimes owned hundreds of horses.

Buffalo

The Cheyenne depended on buffalo for food, shelter, and other daily items. Meat from an average buffalo could produce about 140 pounds (64 kilograms) of dried meat called jerky. One buffalo could feed an adult for about 200 days. A skilled hunter killed two or three buffalo in one hunt.

The Cheyenne dried most of the buffalo meat. Fresh meat lasted only 24 hours before it spoiled. Drying kept the meat from spoiling quickly.

Along with meat, other parts of the buffalo had important uses. Hides served as tepee covers. Hides also were used to make clothing, saddles, ropes, and packs to carry food and

The Cheyenne used horses for transportation and hunting.

Cheyenne women spread buffalo skins on the ground to
work into leather. The women also placed buffalo meat on
racks to dry.

household goods. Buffalo horns and bones were useful for making spoons, cups, and other tools.

Children

The Cheyenne valued their children. The birth of a child increased the number of people in the band. Having more people gave the band a better chance of surviving.

Cheyenne adults were patient in teaching their children. They never hit children for bad behavior. Adults taught children to be respectful and behave well. Adults used stories to teach children how to act. Many stories taught children to be respectful, brave, and generous. Stories also taught Cheyenne history.

Women's Roles

Cheyenne women always had work to do. They took care of the household. They carried water and collected firewood. They made leather, clothing, and tepee covers. When moving camp, women took down the tepees and packed the horses. They put up the tepees when they arrived at a new camp.

Girls worked next to their mothers and learned to prepare foods. They gathered wild turnips and potatoes. The turnips were dried and crushed to make flour. During summer, women gathered ripe elderberries and chokecherries. They taught their daughters to pound chokecherries into small, flat cakes. The cakes were dried in the sun to make hard patties that lasted weeks without spoiling.

During a buffalo hunt, women followed the hunters to collect the meat and hides. Women took the meat back to camp and spread it on drying racks. They worked the hides into leather.

Men's Roles

Young Cheyenne boys trained to become warriors and food providers for their families. Boys learned to ride as soon as they could sit on a horse. When they got older, boys looked after the horses. The boys trained young horses by petting them and playing with them. Boys taught the horses to accept riders on their backs.

When a boy was old enough, a male family member gave him a small bow and arrows. Boys practiced shooting until they could hit a target every time. They hunted rabbits and birds for food.

Starting at about age 12, boys took their first steps toward adulthood. At that age, they were allowed to go on buffalo hunts. Until young men killed their first buffalo, they could

Cheyenne Batter Bread

Before the Cheyenne moved to the Great Plains, their main food was corn. This recipe comes from a time after the Cheyenne moved onto reservations.

Ingredients

4 cups (960 mL) milk
¾ cup (175 mL) honey
2 cups (480 mL) cornmeal
3 egg yolks
4 tablespoons (60 mL) melted butter

1½ teaspoons (7.5 mL) salt
½ teaspoon (2.5 mL) pepper
3 egg whites

Equipment

liquid measuring cups
3-quart (3-liter) saucepan
wooden mixing spoon
medium mixing bowl

egg beater
nonstick cooking spray
2-quart (2-liter) baking dish
oven mitts

What You Do

1. Preheat oven to 375°F (190°C).
2. Pour milk and honey in saucepan. Over medium heat, slowly bring the milk and honey to a boil. Stir constantly so mixture does not burn.
3. Slowly stir in cornmeal. Continue stirring until thick.
4. Mix in egg yolks, butter, salt, and pepper. Remove from heat.
5. In mixing bowl, beat egg whites until they form stiff peaks that stand up straight when you lift the beater. Gently stir egg whites into the corn mixture.
6. Spray a 2-quart (2-liter) baking dish with nonstick cooking spray. Spoon mixture into the baking dish.
7. Bake for 20 to 30 minutes. Bread should be golden brown and puffy when done.

Serves about 8

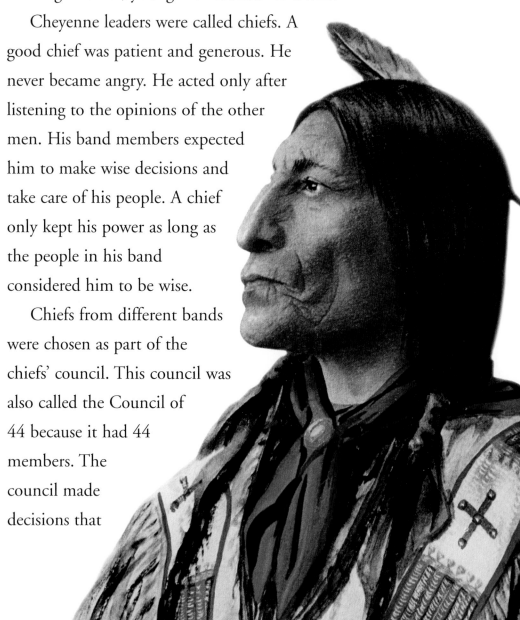

not go to war. Later, after they proved their skill at both hunting and war, young men looked for a wife.

Cheyenne leaders were called chiefs. A good chief was patient and generous. He never became angry. He acted only after listening to the opinions of the other men. His band members expected him to make wise decisions and take care of his people. A chief only kept his power as long as the people in his band considered him to be wise.

Chiefs from different bands were chosen as part of the chiefs' council. This council was also called the Council of 44 because it had 44 members. The council made decisions that

Arrow Makers

The Cheyenne were well known for their fine arrows. Other American Indians traded meat or horses for Cheyenne arrows. Some older Cheyenne men made arrows all year long.

Cherry bush wood was used for arrow shafts. Pieces of a stone called flint were sharpened and used for arrow points. Later, metal and glass were used for points. Turkey feathers were attached to the shaft to help the arrows fly straight.

Plains Indians communicated with each other by using hand signals. The gesture for the Cheyenne was related to their arrows. The sign was made by pulling the right pointer finger across the left pointer finger several times. This gesture meant "striped arrows." The sign referred to the striped turkey feathers attached to Cheyenne arrows.

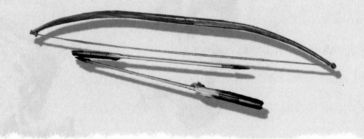

affected all the Cheyenne. The chiefs' council chose four Old Man Chiefs. These men led the council. The council met every year in early summer.

Marriage

When a young woman was ready to be married, her parents looked for a man from a different Cheyenne band. Marriages strengthened relationships between the bands. Young women married between the ages of 16 and 20. Young men usually married in their early 20s.

Weddings involved a large feast and an exchange of gifts between the families. The families exchanged buffalo robes, horses, or guns. When the wedding was done, the couple moved into a new tepee near the bride's parents.

Spiritual Life

Spirits were central to Cheyenne beliefs. The Cheyenne believed that all life came from a spirit called Maheo (muh-HAY-oh). They believed Maheo created the world. The Cheyenne also found spirits in birds, animals, and the earth and sky. People prayed for spiritual power from Maheo or other spirits.

Most Cheyenne men made a vision quest to mountains or other high places. During a vision quest, the men fasted for up to four days. They prayed for the power to solve problems in their families or bands. They hoped to have visions that would show them how to live their lives.

Sweet Medicine and the Arrows

In Cheyenne stories, Sweet Medicine was a man who lived hundreds of years ago. Before he was born, the Cheyenne were unhappy. They lived without laws and often fought with each other.

As a boy, Sweet Medicine argued with a Cheyenne leader over a buffalo hide. The Cheyenne threw him out of camp. While he was gone, he traveled to Bear Butte in South Dakota.

The Cheyenne say spirits at Bear Butte spoke to Sweet Medicine. The spirits gave him laws for the Cheyenne. They also gave him four sacred arrows. Two were for success in war. Two were for success in hunting. The spirits taught Sweet Medicine to pray to the arrows. The spirits taught him to make a special tepee to keep the arrows safe.

After four years, Sweet Medicine returned to the Cheyenne. He brought the four sacred arrows. He taught his people everything he learned from the spirits. He started military societies to protect the Cheyenne and enforce the laws he learned.

The Cheyenne still celebrate the Arrow Ceremony. It renews the power that Sweet Medicine brought to his people. An Arrow Keeper with the Southern Cheyenne protects the sacred arrows. He keeps them inside a special tepee.

Cheyenne Sun Dancers painted their bodies to prepare for the Sun Dance ceremony.

One of the most important sacred places for the Cheyenne was a steep, flat mountain in South Dakota called Bear Butte. At Bear Butte, Cheyenne holy man Sweet Medicine had learned how the Cheyenne should act. He taught the Cheyenne what he had learned.

Ceremonies

Each year, the Cheyenne gathered for the Arrow Ceremony. The Cheyenne believe Maheo gave four arrows to Sweet Medicine. Sweet Medicine gave the arrows to the Cheyenne people. The Cheyenne believe the arrows bring power to feed and protect their people. The Arrow Ceremony renewed the power of the sacred arrows.

After the Arrow Ceremony, the Cheyenne celebrated the Sun Dance. This ceremony included prayers for new grass to grow for the animals. Some male dancers pierced their skin with hooks or thorns tied to a tree. They fasted and danced for several days. Their goal was to have visions that would help their people. The Arrow Ceremony and Sun Dance lasted four days each. The Cheyenne still practice the Arrow Ceremony and the Sun Dance.

Ceremonies strengthened Cheyenne relationships with each other. People visited with each other, traded between bands, and looked for marriage partners for their children at ceremonies.

American Indians hunted buffalo on the Great Plains.
Change came to the Cheyenne when they traded for
horses to help them hunt on the Great Plains.

Chapter Three

Change Comes to the Cheyenne

In the 1700s, the Cheyenne traded with other plains Indians for horses. Horses allowed them to travel farther to hunt. The Cheyenne began to hunt on Lakota Sioux, Blackfeet, and Comanche hunting grounds. These nations fought the Cheyenne to protect their hunting rights and trade relationships.

As the Cheyenne moved onto the Great Plains, they needed to protect themselves from other Indians. The Cheyenne joined another small nation, the Arapaho, in an alliance. This friendly relationship strengthened both groups. The alliance helped them control trade from present-day

Wyoming to present-day Oklahoma. The Cheyenne and Arapaho traded buffalo hides for horses from Indians of the American Southwest. They traded for guns and tools from northern plains Indians.

Trails and Change

In 1821, white settlers began to travel west along the Santa Fe Trail. This trading route started in Missouri and continued to Santa Fe, New Mexico. The trail passed through Cheyenne territory. The Cheyenne began to have closer contact with white traders and settlers.

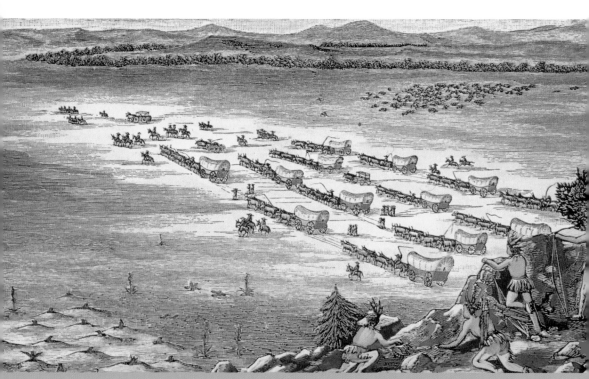

American Indians watched as white settlers traveled along the Santa Fe Trail.

Brothers William and Charles Bent built Bent's Fort along the Santa Fe Trail in southern Colorado. The Cheyenne brought buffalo skins to this trading post. They traded the skins for kettles, guns, bullets, beads, and food.

Starting in the 1840s, settlers began to travel along a trail north of Bent's Fort. This route was the Oregon Trail. It ran from western Missouri to the Rocky Mountains. Thousands of settlers followed the trail to Oregon and California. In 1848, the discovery of gold in California drew thousands more people west along the trail.

The heavy traffic on the Oregon Trail divided the buffalo into northern and southern herds. To hunt, the Cheyenne also divided into northern and southern groups. The Southern Cheyenne ranged south from Denver, Colorado, to Oklahoma. The Northern Cheyenne hunted north of Denver.

By 1850, many settlers lived along the Platte River and in Denver. The settlers wanted to claim Cheyenne land. Gold was discovered in Colorado in 1859. Thousands of miners and settlers entered Cheyenne land to mine the gold.

The settlers and miners took away Cheyenne land and sources of food. They killed thousands of buffalo. By 1861, many Cheyenne were starving. Some warriors stole cattle for food. The warriors attacked settlers who tried to stop them.

In 1861, Southern Cheyenne chiefs signed the Treaty of Fort Wise. This agreement placed the Southern Cheyenne on a reservation in southern Colorado. Many Cheyenne leaders did not agree to the treaty. They continued to hunt and camp where they wished. Their actions led to fights between Cheyenne warriors and U.S. soldiers.

Problems grew between the U.S. Army and the Cheyenne. In the spring of 1864, soldiers entered the Cheyenne reservation looking for horse thieves. They found Chief Lean Bear and Chief Black Kettle's village. Lean Bear met the soldiers. He carried a peace medal he had received from the U.S. government. Without waiting to listen to Lean Bear, the soldiers shot him and attacked the other Cheyenne.

The attack angered the Cheyenne warriors. In revenge, they killed settlers, soldiers, and travelers. The warriors kept mail and supplies from reaching Denver.

Colorado Governor John Evans ordered all Cheyenne to travel to the nearest military fort. He said the government would protect any Cheyenne who reported. Black Kettle brought his group to Fort Lyons. The fort commander told him to camp at nearby Sand Creek. Black Kettle felt safe under army protection.

About the time the Cheyenne camped, the Colorado military commander ordered Colonel John Chivington to attack them. In late November 1864, about 700 Colorado volunteer

Military Societies

When a young Cheyenne man approached adulthood, he joined a military society. Military societies were similar to police forces. They protected the Cheyenne in times of war. They also kept order during large hunts and gatherings. The man shown in this photo belongs to the Dog Soldier society.

Young men usually joined their fathers' society. They started in the societies by performing small tasks. First, young men held warriors' horses during battles. Later, they were allowed to join in the fights.

Every four years, society members chose chiefs from their warriors. The chiefs led the military society in battles.

Several military societies still exist today. They help keep large gatherings peaceful. They act as police during powwows. They also raise money to help their members take part in ceremonies.

soldiers attacked Black Kettle's camp. This attack became known as the Sand Creek Massacre. As the soldiers attacked, Black Kettle raised a white flag and an American flag. He hoped to show that the Cheyenne and Arapaho in camp were peaceful.

Black Kettle (1803?–1868)

Black Kettle was a Cheyenne chief. He was probably born in 1803. Nothing is known about his life until the 1860s.

As an adult, Black Kettle preferred peace to war. He signed the 1861 Treaty of Fort Wise. In it, he agreed not to fight. Instead, he led a group of Cheyenne and Arapaho to a small reservation in southern Colorado.

Americans did not always notice Black Kettle's peace efforts. In spite of his flags of peace, U.S. soldiers attacked the Cheyenne and Arapaho camped at Sand Creek in Colorado. The soldiers' actions angered Cheyenne warriors. The warriors attacked wagon trains, towns, and U.S. soldiers. As a result, the soldiers increased their attacks against the Cheyenne.

Black Kettle continued to work for peace for his people. In 1867, he signed another peace treaty. The Treaty of Medicine Lodge gave the Cheyenne a new reservation in Indian Territory.

Other Cheyenne continued their attacks, but Black Kettle remained peaceful. In 1868, George Custer led what was later called the Battle of the Washita. About 800 U.S. soldiers attacked Black Kettle's group at the Washita River in Indian Territory. The soldiers killed Black Kettle and many other Cheyenne and Arapaho.

John Metcalf

The soldiers ignored the flags. They killed about 150 men, women, and children. Black Kettle and some others escaped to join family in Kansas.

News of the attack spread quickly among the Cheyenne and their allies. They wanted to fight back. In January 1865, more than 1,000 warriors attacked American settlements along the Platte River.

The U.S. government said the Sand Creek Massacre was wrong, and that it was sorry for the deaths. The government hoped the Cheyenne would stop their attacks, but they did not.

Some Cheyenne still wanted peace. In 1867, Black Kettle and other southern leaders signed the Treaty of Medicine Lodge. This treaty created a new Cheyenne-Arapaho reservation in Indian Territory. Indian Territory later became the state of Oklahoma.

Hard Times in the North

The U.S. government believed the Northern Cheyenne should follow the Treaty of Medicine Lodge. It wanted them to move from Wyoming to the Indian Territory. Instead, the Northern Cheyenne and Northern Arapaho joined their former enemies the Lakota Sioux. Together, these people closed routes into Montana and Wyoming to keep out American settlers.

In 1868, the Cheyenne, Lakota, and other Indians signed the Treaty of Fort Laramie. In this treaty, the U.S. government promised to keep whites out of the Black Hills of South Dakota.

When gold was discovered in the Black Hills, miners and settlers came to the area. The Cheyenne and their allies kept them out of the Black Hills. As a result, the U.S. government declared war on the Indians.

In June 1876, General George Custer and 254 soldiers began the Battle of the Little Big Horn. They attacked more than 2,000 Cheyenne, Arapaho, and Lakota. The warriors were camped along the Little Big Horn River in Montana. They fought back, killing Custer and his men. The warriors then split into small groups to escape other soldiers in the area.

In and Out of Indian Territory

Angry soldiers followed the Cheyenne through Montana. Whenever they could, they burned Cheyenne camps. They destroyed food and shelter. In 1877, the Northern Cheyenne surrendered. They were sent to live with the Southern Cheyenne in Indian Territory.

Conditions were poor in Indian Territory. The government had promised the Northern Cheyenne food and clothing. But not enough food was available to feed both the Southern and Northern Cheyenne. Many Cheyenne became sick. The Northern Cheyenne asked to return to their northern land. The U.S. government refused.

In 1878, Chief Dull Knife and Chief Little Wolf decided to leave the reservation. They and 300 Northern Cheyenne planned to travel almost 1,000 miles (1,600 kilometers) north to Montana and Wyoming. The group split in two, believing the soldiers would have trouble following them north.

Soldiers captured Dull Knife's group soon after they left Indian Territory. The soldiers took them to Fort Robinson in Nebraska. The army planned to return Dull Knife's group south to Indian Territory.

Dull Knife's group then escaped

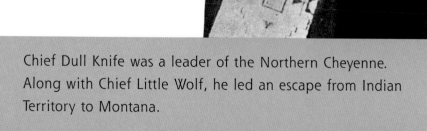

Chief Dull Knife was a leader of the Northern Cheyenne. Along with Chief Little Wolf, he led an escape from Indian Territory to Montana.

from Fort Robinson. Soldiers killed and recaptured many of Dull Knife's group on their way north. Still, he and a few others reached the Lakota Indians at the Pine Ridge Reservation in South Dakota.

Little Wolf's group traveled north to Montana. In 1879, soldiers captured the group. The soldiers took the Cheyenne to Fort Keogh in Montana and held them there.

In 1884, the U.S. government created a reservation for the Northern Cheyenne in southwestern Montana. More than 1,200 Cheyenne from Montana, Wyoming, South Dakota, and Indian Territory moved to the reservation.

New Laws Bring More Change

In 1887, the U.S. government passed the General Allotment Act. This law allowed the government to begin splitting up reservations. Indians were supposed to choose small pieces of land called allotments for individually owned farms. The government sold any leftover land or gave it to settlers.

In 1892, the government forced the Southern Cheyenne and Arapaho to divide their land. They lost most of their reservation. Each family had to choose 160 acres (65 hectares) of land for individual farms. The U.S. government opened the leftover land to white settlers.

The U.S. government also took away the Cheyenne's right to govern themselves. The government sent Indian agents who were supposed to help the Cheyenne. The Cheyenne and other Indian nations were under U.S. control for many years.

The U.S. government passed the Indian Reorganization Act in 1934. This law restored self-government to many Indian nations. It also returned some of the land taken away under the General Allotment Act.

A Southern Cheyenne family posed outside their home in Indian Territory. By the mid-1890s, Southern Cheyenne and Arapaho families had moved onto individual allotments of land.

Cheyenne teenagers are like other teenagers across the United States. They enjoy having fun with their friends.

Chapter Four

The Cheyenne Today

Distance separates the Southern and Northern Cheyenne. The Southern Cheyenne headquarters is located in Oklahoma. The Northern Cheyenne are based in southern Montana.

The Southern Cheyenne

In 1936, the Southern Cheyenne and Arapaho formed a tribal government. Each nation elects four representatives to the Business Committee. The committee manages tribal land.

Today, the Southern Cheyenne and Arapaho live in Concho, Oklahoma. They control about 10,000 acres (4,047 hectares) of the 3 million acres (1,214,000 hectares) they had before allotment.

Finding jobs is a challenge for the Cheyenne. Southern Cheyenne farms and ranches cannot support large families. To help, the tribal government offers job training. But after training, many Cheyenne must leave the area to find work.

Education is important to the Southern Cheyenne. Head Start is a preschool program offered to children ages 3 to 5. Southern Cheyenne children attend public schools in the Concho area. The tribal government provides scholarships for students to attend colleges or universities.

The Northern Cheyenne

The Northern Cheyenne government is called the Tribal Council. The council has 19 members. Each member represents about 200 Northern Cheyenne. Council members elect a president who serves for four years. Council headquarters are located in Lame Deer, Montana.

Many Northern Cheyenne can find jobs. They work for Cheyenne services or schools. Other people work off the reservation. Cheyenne work for mining companies, sawmills, and the Montana Power Company. Other Cheyenne are lawyers, ranchers, and politicians.

Land development is an important issue for the Northern Cheyenne. For example, in the 1960s, coal was discovered beneath Northern Cheyenne land. Some Cheyenne wanted to protect the land from strip mining. Others wanted to allow mining. They believed mining would bring jobs and money to the reservation. The Tribal Council decided not to allow the coal to be mined. They were concerned that mining might pollute the air, land, and water.

The Northern Cheyenne value education. The reservation houses two Indian schools. A religious group called the St. Labre Catholic Mission runs the schools. Students range from kindergarten through grade 12. Along with other subjects, students learn Cheyenne language and culture. Chief Dull Knife College in Lame Deer offers two-year degrees to students. Offering academic classes since 1978, the college also provides vocational training. Students also learn Cheyenne cultural values.

Children learn about Cheyenne language, customs, and traditions at ceremonies and reservation schools.

Many Cheyenne continue their traditions by dancing in powwows and wearing regalia.

Chapter Five

Sharing the Traditions

The Cheyenne want to share their history and culture with other people. Many Cheyenne do so through their art. Some Cheyenne decorate clothing with bright beadwork as their ancestors have done for hundreds of years. Artists make moccasins or other traditional clothing. Some painters create pictures of Cheyenne life and traditions.

The Cheyenne continue their traditions by attending powwows. Southern Cheyenne host more than 250 small powwows in Oklahoma each year. These gatherings celebrate special family occasions. The family hosting the powwow gives food and gifts to their guests. Dancing follows the gift-giving.

Both Northern and Southern Cheyenne dance in large powwows around the United States. Various Indian nations sponsor these powwows. Indian dancers from all over North America compete for prize money. Tourists and other guests are welcome to watch.

The Cheyenne also continue their traditions by teaching their children the Cheyenne language. Chief Dull Knife College offers classes in Cheyenne. It also offers classes in Cheyenne storytelling. The Southern Cheyenne offer language courses that satisfy high school foreign language requirements. Internet sites offer tapes and dictionaries of the Cheyenne language.

Looking to the Past and Future

In May 2002, a business owner in Minnesota bought a Colorado ranch. The land included the site of the Sand Creek Massacre. The man gave the site to the Cheyenne and Arapaho. With the help of the National Park Service, the Cheyenne and Arapaho plan to create a national historic site at Sand Creek. They are eager to visit and care for the place where so many Cheyenne and Arapaho died.

The Cheyenne look with hope to the future. They have survived wars, disease, and mistreatment. They remain a proud, strong people. They know they will always have a place in the world.

Suzan Shown Harjo (1945-)

Suzan Shown Harjo is a member of the Southern Cheyenne and Arapaho. She grew up in a poor family on a farm in Oklahoma. When Suzan was 12 until she was 16, her family lived in Italy. Her father was stationed at an army base there.

During the 1960s, Harjo moved to New York City. There, she entered the news and entertainment industry. She became a news reporter, actress, and radio producer. She enjoyed her work but wanted to do more to help American Indians.

In 1974, Harjo moved to Washington, D.C., and became involved with Indian rights. In 1978, President Jimmy Carter asked her to work with the U.S. government. In her work, she helped write laws to protect Indian land. She also worked for the National Congress of American Indians to protect Indian rights. In 1984, Harjo created the Morning Star Institute. This Washington, D.C., organization protects sacred Indian land. It also promotes Indian arts and culture.

Harjo has lived much of her life helping American Indians. She continues to make people aware of health, civil rights, and unemployment problems among Indians.

Cheyenne Timeline

The Treaty of Fort Wise places the Southern Cheyenne on a Colorado reservation.

The Sand Creek Massacre takes place in Colorado.

Chief Black Kettle is killed at the Battle of the Washita.

About 1800   1861   1864   1868   1876

The Cheyenne become nomadic buffalo hunters on the Great Plains.

Cheyenne, Arapaho and Lakota warriors defeat General George Custer's forces at the Battle of the Little Big Hor

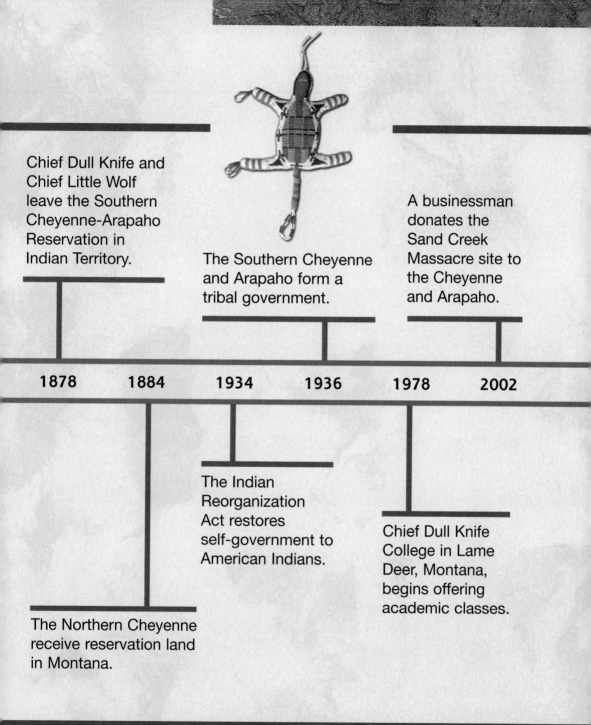

Chief Dull Knife and Chief Little Wolf leave the Southern Cheyenne-Arapaho Reservation in Indian Territory.

The Southern Cheyenne and Arapaho form a tribal government.

A businessman donates the Sand Creek Massacre site to the Cheyenne and Arapaho.

1878   1884   1934   1936   1978   2002

The Indian Reorganization Act restores self-government to American Indians.

Chief Dull Knife College in Lame Deer, Montana, begins offering academic classes.

The Northern Cheyenne receive reservation land in Montana.

Glossary

alliance (uh-LYE-uhnss)—an agreement among groups to work together

allotment (uh-LOT-muhnt)—a plot of land that heads of American Indian families received when the U.S. government divided reservation land

butte (BYOOT)—a rocky hill with steep sides and a flat top that stands by itself

fast (FAST)—to go without food for a long period of time

nomadic (noh-MAD-ik)—traveling from place to place in search of food and water

Internet Sites

Do you want to find out more about the Cheyenne? Let FactHound, our fact-finding hound dog, do the research for you.

Here's how:
1) Visit *http://www.facthound.com*.
2) Type in the **Book ID** number: **0736821783**.
3) Click on **FETCH IT**.

FactHound will fetch Internet sites picked by our editors just for you!

Places to Write and Visit

Black Kettle Museum
P.O. Box 252
U.S. Highway 283 and State Highway 47
Cheyenne, OK 73628-0252

Cheyenne and Arapaho Tribes of Oklahoma
P.O. Box 38
Concho, OK 73022

Little Bighorn Battlefield National Monument
P.O. Box 39
Exit 510 Off I-90 and Highway 212
Crow Agency, MT 59022-0039

Northern Cheyenne Reservation
P.O. Box 128
Lame Deer, MT 59043

For Further Reading

Bial, Raymond. *The Cheyenne.* Lifeways. New York: Benchmark Books, 2001.

Remington, Gwen. *The Cheyenne.* Indigenous Peoples of North America. San Diego: Lucent Books, 2001.

Sita, Lisa. *Indians of the Great Plains: Traditions, History, Legends, and Life.* Native Americans. Milwaukee: Gareth Stevens, 2000.

Index